I'll Never Be Broke Another Day In My Life

Real Answers to
Financial Hardship

Leroy Thompson

First Printing 2001

ISBN 0-9632584-7-8

Ever Increasing Word Ministries
P.O. Box 7
Darrow, Louisiana 70725

Contents

Introduction

When President George W. Bush was sworn into office, I attended an inaugural luncheon. One of President Bush's assistants had invited me, and as I listened to one of the speakers, he said something that really caught my attention.

As this speaker talked, he made reference to people who have faith and who love God. But then, almost in passing, he said the Church was "part of those whom prosperity had left behind."

Sadly enough, that speaker's words were more true than he realized.

The Church — the children of God, the chosen ones of the Most High — has been left behind. . . singing, dancing, praying and preaching. . . with no money.

While we stand around singing, "Amazing Grace How Sweet the Sound That Saved a Wretch

Like Me. . . " the rest of the world is gathering up and enjoying all the money and goods of this earth.

My brother and sister, it's time that changed. It's time we elevated ourselves. It's time we educated our spirits. It's time we reclaimed what rightfully belongs to us.

That's why I have written this book. I want to educate your spirit. I want to see you prosper as God intended.

God did not create you to live broke and do without. He didn't create you to live in lack, never having enough money, never having all your needs met. And He especially never intended His Church to be left behind while the world gathered up all the money.

No. He intended for wealth to come to you by your becoming a spiritually educated man or woman. Not intellectually educated. Not a philosopher, or someone with degrees from an institution of higher learning. No, I'm talking about educating your spirit — or, as the Bible calls it — renewing your mind.

I am an educated man. My spirit is filled with education. My mind has been renewed. I know how to have money. I have plenty of it, and I got it all by the Spirit. . . not by my mind.

Oh, I remember the days when I worked two jobs and my wife worked one. I also remember that no matter how hard the both of us worked, we were never able just to catch up. Yet, I remember being spiritually ignorant in those days, too. I was spiritually deceived. But thank God, the Holy Spirit got hold of me and started educating me according to the ways and Word of God.

You see, for far too long, most Church people have been deceived. The devil has deceived the Church about money. And, yes, if you're broke right now, you're deceived, too. You're living under the curse. You're living under the devil's control.

How do I know that?

Because if you were living under the covenant of God afforded you by the blood of Jesus, you would not be broke.

Jesus made it pretty plain when He declared, "I am come that [you] might have life, and that [you] might have it more abundantly" (John 10:10). You are supposed to have more. That's the truth Jesus spoke.

The bottom line is, it's not right for you as a child of God to go through the same struggles the rest of this world does. It's not right for you to be living under the pressures of not having enough money. . . living from paycheck to paycheck. . . and everybody in your household working two jobs — including your dog!

The world does it because they're living purely out of the flesh. They're living like the natural men that they are.

You, however, are not purely natural — not if you are born again. You are Spirit-filled. You are Spirit-led. You function under the anointing of

God. You have God-given covenant rights, and part of those rights involve money, provision, goods, and so on.

In short, money is supposed to obey you, not control you. Money is not your master. On the contrary. When you speak, money should do what you tell it to do — just as the fig tree obeyed Jesus (Mark 11), just as the sea obeyed Him (Mark 4), just as He said the "mountain" would obey us (Matthew 21).

The coming of our Lord Jesus Christ is very soon, and we have a lot of work to do. Billions of people are on their way to hell and they need to be born again. But it's going to take money to get the job done.

God wants His people prosperous and wealthy so we can establish His covenant in the earth, so whatever aspect of the gospel He needs to get to people, He can call on us to get it done. Having money is far more than owning houses and cars.

Still, Isaiah 1:19 promises that, "If ye be willing and obedient, ye shall eat the good of the land."

The good of the land is money. If you don't have money, you cannot eat the good of the land. You can be as spiritual as you want to be, but without money, you cannot drive the nice cars, live in the nice houses, dress in nice clothes or eat at nice restaurants.

God's will for us as believers is revealed quite clearly in Psalm 66:12.

"Thou hast caused men to ride over our heads; we went through fire and through water: but thou broughtest us out into a *wealthy place.*"

God brought them out. . . and He will bring you out, too. Out of debt, out of lack, out of barely getting by. He will bring you out of it *into* a wealthy place, a place where you can dominate financially. A place where every need is met, every desire fulfilled, every dream brought to pass.

To reach that place, you must educate your spirit man and purpose to lay hold of what is rightfully yours.

If you are a born again believer, you have the same Spirit within you as I do. It is that Spirit that will educate you.

Draw on that Holy Spirit residing on the inside of you. Draw on the Spirit that resides in me and on the anointed pages of this book. That Spirit that will produce an anointing such that you will never have to be concerned about money another day in your life.

As you read this book and I unfold the Word of God to you by the Holy Spirit, a debt-destroying, lack-removing anointing will come upon you and deliver you.

What's more, supernatural favor will come on you because of that anointing. Things will start happening for you, opportunities will open up to you, opportunities that were not available to you before.

So read each word carefully. Meditate on it. Then apply it. . . apply it. . . apply it. As you do, your spirit will become educated and soon you'll be able to declare with absolute confidence:

"I'LL NEVER BE BROKE ANOTHER DAY IN MY LIFE!"

Leroy Thompson
August 2001

What Will You Do
When the System Shuts Down?

1 chapter

What Will
You Do
When the
System Shuts
Down?

Not long ago, I was reading the newspaper when I came across a story of a lady who made $600 a month, and her utility bill totaled $545. Needless to say she was in a panic.

Her story, however, is not unique. In fact, it reflects our entire economic system. And in case you haven't heard: Recession is coming.

I'm not prophesying a recession. All you have to do is open your eyes and look around at how people in the finance sector, the business sector and political sector are messing up. Oh, everyone's acting like they know what they're doing. But they don't.

Truthfully, though, whether or not they know what they're doing doesn't matter. . . not to born-again, Spirit-filled, children of God.

For us, the question is. . . *What are we doing?*

To begin with, if you are depending on your savings for security, you can forget it. That little stash of money you've been saving for 40 years won't cut it. Recession can eat it up in no time. Even if your house is paid for and you have $100,000 in the bank, it just takes the right kind of recession to hit, the economy to go crazy and you can say "Bye-bye" to everything you have counted on your whole lifetime.

Besides all that, God doesn't want you dependent on your little stash of cash, or whatever you're depending on as a safety net. He wants you in a position that *no matter what comes,* you know Who your source is, and you will prosper.

Recession 101

In simple terms, recession is when there's a *shortage.* A recession hits and the system goes bust and people go crazy, including religious folks.

As I was seeking the Lord about all this recently, He arrested my attention by asking me a question. . .

What are **you** *going to do when the system shuts down?* He asked.

Well, if you think about it, even from a biblical standpoint, that's not some make-believe question. It is a startling reality that demands a *real* answer.

For example, we have record of the "world's system" shutting down in ancient Egypt. In Joseph's days, everything shut down completely due to famine. Prior to the disaster, though, Joseph had a word from the Lord, a directive from God to store up. Joseph listened to God and obeyed, and consequently, saved a nation from starving (Genesis 39).

Genesis 26 tells of another famine. Abraham's son, Isaac, was walking under a financial anointing and heard from God in all of his financial matters. At one point, the Lord actually told Isaac to sow during a famine. . . and the harvest Isaac reaped was a hundredfold (verse 12).

Both of these men of God were blessed in the middle of a system shut-down because they knew how to follow the direction of God in financial matters.

Just like them, you have to know how to hear from God in these days — recession, or no recession. Yet, even in the middle of the world's worst recession, there can be restoration. And true restoration is when the wealth of God's people is restored to them.

In fact, I'll even dare to take that truth a step a further:

Recession *will* occur so restoration *can* occur.

Did you get that?

I truly believe that recession is coming so there can be restoration to the Body of Christ.

Revival is about to come on the scene. And this revival — this end-time harvest of souls — will require everything that rightfully belongs to the Body of Christ be restored to her.

Why?

For one simple reason: Because revival is about to come on the scene. And this revival — this end-time harvest of souls — will require everything that rightfully belongs to the Body of Christ to be restored to her.

You see, God wants His Church busy about His business, not busy about trying to make a living, day after day.

People are so busy trying to make a living, trying to keep up with the pace of life (never mind trying to keep up with the Joneses anymore,) that we all have begun to recognize that something is going wrong.

It's time for a revelation. Religious folks are never going to make it through what's ahead. They

can shout and jump while everybody is getting a little prosperity, but when reces-
sion and famine hit, when the
system shuts down, religion is
not going to help them. And

*It's time for a revela-
tion. Religious folks
are never going to
make it through what's
ahead.*

when that day arrives, fear will come into town by
the truckloads.

What can save them?

Revelation of God's Word—revelation of the
Word and your being prosperous and rich.

Beware of False Foundations

The first step in spiritual education is establishing a correct foundation. . . a correct understanding
of how we are to live as Christians, trusting God
and looking to Him for answers. But before we lay
that foundation, I want to expose some of the false
foundations upon which we often base our lives.

In general, we've already seen that we cannot
live according to the world's standards. The prob-

lem with that is the world is living under the curse (Deuteronomy 28). They're not walking in accordance with a covenant of Almighty God. They're living after the flesh. They live according to the limitations of this earth, or natural, realm. We, however, are called to something much higher and far greater.

The Spirit of God recently spoke to me saying, "Tell [the people], He who lives by donation cannot dominate." And by *donation*, He was referring to handouts from the government.

The government will try and donate some things to you, and you will have to choose whether or not to receive it. There is nothing wrong with being on Government assistance, if you need help. I am just saying don't stay there. Make a decision to let God be your source.

Let me warn you, though, there are some things on the horizon. The government will offer money to churches, and a lot of them will jump on it. In the end, however, it will lead to bondage and the church will no longer be free.

Actually, to be frank with you, I see the Church being put under politics and the government. It won't be long before the government will be telling Christians how to pray. And from there it will only get worse.

The government cannot be your source. Make sure you are not relying on the government. Just like the lady with the utility bill, the government won't pay you enough for what you need. . . but God can!

And if God can handle what He's called the Church to do, then what's the point of turning to the government, or anyone else, for that matter?

As Christians living in this world, we can also tend to base our lives on *seasons*. Certainly, there are the obvious seasons in this world, yet, our lives must not be based on them. By that I mean, we can not live according to everything that's happening around us in this temporal realm.

Over the years, I have also watched as Christians explained their compromising lifestyles by talking about *cycles*. Cycles in the world's system that come and go. One day they're on top of the world. The next day, they've bottomed out.

Well, let me give you a revelation. Those kinds of up-and-down graphs don't belong to the Church—not if you believe, *"The Lord is my Shepard I shall not want"* (Psalm 23). Not if you believe, *"My God shall supply all my needs according to His riches in glory by Christ Jesus"* (Philippians 4:19).

You either compromise, or you are fully convinced. There's nothing in between.

Personally, I'm fully convinced the covenant is right. I'm fully convinced that God is at work doing some things on our behalf.

But know this: When you recognize that God is at work, busy doing good things for you, people will come along and persecute you because of it. And when that happens, you cannot act like a coward and quit—all because you're so concerned about how other people feel. No. You cannot base your life on what you *think* other people might say about you. Don't even give it another thought, just press on.

Finally, another false foundation is one that we as believers face within our own circle. We call them *waves*.

You've probably seen or heard about these different *waves* that have come washing over the Body of Christ. You could call it the *latest Christian craze*. A new wave hits and people in the church jump right on in to what's popular among the brethren. . . and then they turn and walk right back out. They get a little "touch" of the wave, like joy, for example. And when it passes on, they stand around waiting for the next one.

This is not characteristic of God. And that's not how He operates. Remember, it was God Who said, "I am the Lord and I change not" (Malachi 3:6).

So, you can be sure that there are no up-and-down meters or passing fads in glory. The meters and the trends only move one way in the kingdom of God. . . *Up*. And if you really believe that, you will not live according to any kind of cycle. You will not live based on any passing wave or short-lived season. You will not base your life on what the government says, or what anyone else might think. You will establish yourself on your covenant with Almighty God.

The Meaning of "Blessed"

To be truly free of the world's system—it's seasons, waves and cycles—you have to train yourself to live by the covenant, that is, by the Word of God. You have to become established on the Word. You have to be determined in your spirit that whatever it says is what you're going to have, no matter what. And once you make that decision, you *will* increase. . . even when the world's system shuts down.

Psalm 105 recounts for us how God delivered the people of Israel from being enslaved to Egypt and its pharaoh—the world-system of their day.

Verse 37 says, "He [God] brought them forth also with silver and gold: and there was not one feeble person among their tribes."

Notice that the first word is *He,* referring to God. That's the key to this whole revelation of never being broke another day in your life.

God is the only One Who can bring us out of debt and lack. . . and keep us out!

When no one else knows what to do, there is *He*. But you have to know it. And you have to be confident that *He* will do it for *you*.

If anyone could have stopped these Israelites from getting away—particularly with all that gold and silver—it would have been pharaoh. But he couldn't. No one could. Why? Because it was *He* — God — Who was doing the delivering.

But it wasn't just that *He* "brought them forth. . . ."

No. It says, "He brought them forth *also* with silver and gold: and there was *not one* feeble person among their tribes."

In other words, God did it up in style. Everyone came out rich, healthy and whole.

If you're going to bring me out of bondage. . . then bring mc!

Make it so I don't have to be broke another day in my life!

And that's exactly what God did. Psalm 66:12 puts it this way:

"Thou hast caused men to ride over our heads; we went through fire and through water: *but thou broughtest us out into a wealthy place.*"

When it comes down to this money thing, the Church has indeed been through fire and water over it. Consequently, everyone gets nervous every time the preacher starts talking about money. . . everyone but God.

It was God Who told Abraham, "I will make of thee a great nation, and I will bless thee, and make thy name great; and thou shalt be a blessing: And I will bless them that bless thee, and curse him that curseth thee: and in thee shall all families of the earth be blessed" (Genesis 12:2-3).

Here, the word *blessed* means "empowered to prosper."

God was telling Abraham, "I'm going to empower you to prosper until all the nations are empowered to prosper through you." That's just the way God thinks.

But now, the condition for Abraham to receive that much empowerment to prosper was that he "come out."

God told him, "Get thee out of thy country, and from thy kindred, and from thy father's house, unto a land that I will shew thee" (Genesis 12:1).

Sometimes you have to "come out" to be free. You have to come out from the old ways, or everybody else's ways, of doing things and stretch your

Sometimes you have to "come out" to be free. You have to come out from the old ways, or everybody else's ways, of doing things and stretch your wings.

wings. And that's what Abraham did. He obeyed God and came out.

What was the result?

Genesis 13 tells us that Abraham "was very rich in cattle, in silver, and in gold. . . " and that his "substance was great" (verses 2 and 6).

See, we're not talking about what you can do, here. We're not talking about *your* job, or your abilities. We're talking about covenant. But, you have to be willing to be obedient to do whatever that covenant tells you to do.

A lot of people won't budge an inch when God tells them to move.

"No, You don't understand, Lord. . . I've got it worked out and I'll be just fine here the rest of my life."

But the Lord says, *I'm not blessing here.*

Ask me how I know. I had that same "Abraham call." God called me out. Out from my family. Out from my old, comfortable church. And if I had not obeyed God, I wouldn't be where I am today. I sure wouldn't be rich. I'd still be in the land of not enough, the land of broke.

Today, however, I'm in a place where my covenant with God will not let me go broke.

Either we believe 2 Corinthians 8:9, or we don't!

"For ye know the grace [favor] of our Lord Jesus Christ, that, though he was rich, yet for your sakes he became poor, that *ye through his poverty might be rich.*"

For ye know. . . .

Do we know, Church? Do we know Jesus became poor so we could be rich?

Then it's time we looked like it. It's time we acted like it.

Second Corinthians 8:9 is saying, "I'll never be broke another day in my life!"

Psalm 23:1 — "The Lord is my shepherd; I shall not want. . . " — is saying, "I'll never be broke another day in my life!"

Philippians 4:19 — "But my God shall supply all your need. . . " — is saying, "I'll never be broke another day in my life!"

But to live that way every day of your life you may have to snatch yourself out of some circles of friends, family, associations, and become independent of the circumstances around you in order to hear what God is saying to you. That's the only way you'll ever get established in your covenant with God.

We're not living by cycles, or seasons, or waves. We don't live by what the President says, or what Congress says, or what Wall Street says. We're not living according to the world's—or even the religious world's—ups and downs. No. We're living by a covenant with Almighty God. And our God is forever the same. He never changes. . . and neither does His Word.

Psalm 102:13 tells us that God will arise and "have mercy upon Zion: for the time to favour her [that's you and me], yea, the set time, is come."

My brother and sister, your set time is come. The time for God to arise on your behalf has come. And He is going to rise through revelation, and through people receiving it. That's the way God works. God works through revelation. He works through His Word. He works through the anointing.

Abraham had the money. Job had the money. Joseph had the money. And on and on it goes throughout the Old and New covenants.

Now, it's our time.

I'm about to prove to you that it has been — and always will be — God's intention for His children to have the money. It is God, the Heavenly Father, Who intends for us to never be broke another day in our lives.

Go ahead—shout it out loud!

I'LL NEVER BE BROKE ANOTHER DAY IN MY LIFE!

Remember, that's not some cute phrase Leroy Thompson came up with to go preach around the world. No, it was God. It was *His* revelation for *His* Church, today.

So take "I'll never be broke another day in my life!" as a word from Him. And when it rises up in your spirit — say it.

It was Jesus, not Leroy Thompson, Who said, "If you say something, and don't doubt in your heart. . . but believe. . . what you say will come to pass" (Mark 11:23-24).

What's more, it is Jesus Who will bring you out. He'll bring you out with silver and gold. He'll bring you out into that wealthy place in Him.

Money With A Mission

2 chapter

Money With
A Mission

When you talk about supernatural increase, one of the greatest concerns that rises up in the minds of people is "How?" How is God going to prosper me? How is He going to get the money to me?

If you start letting your mind deal with the matter of *how* He will deliver you out of lack, then you will miss the whole point of God's revelation: "I'll Never Be Broke Another Day In My Life."

Besides, if you start dealing with "How?" then you're actually trying to figure out some way to make it happen yourself. You're trying to help God, and He doesn't want your help. He doesn't need your help.

Mark 4:26-27 helps keep our financial deliverance in perspective.

"And he said, So is the kingdom of God, as if a man should cast seed into the ground; And should sleep, and rise night and day, and the seed should spring and grow up, *he knoweth not how.*"

We *knoweth not how* . . . and God doesn't expect us to know.

So, don't waste time baffling and confounding yourself about how your prosperity is going to happen. It's not your business to know how it will happen. What's more, it's not your business how it will happen in your neighbor's life, either. So don't even challenge them. Never challenge someone who is standing on God's Word.

The truth is, this revelation—"I'll Never Be Broke Another Day In My Life!"—is not just about money. It deals with the entire spectrum of God's kingdom. And once you get beyond "I don't know how God's going to do this . . ." you're on your way.

As I said at the end of the last chapter, this revelation is not some cute saying coined by Leroy Thompson. It's a revelation from heaven. . . a Word from God. So, accept that you don't have to know how your financial deliverance will happen. Just let the revelation of it — the reality of it — seep down into your spirit . . . and for once just stop thinking about your bills.

Now, going back to Mark 4, the next two verses are powerful:

"For the earth bringeth forth fruit of herself; first the blade, then the ear, after that the full corn in the ear. But when the fruit is brought forth, immediately he putteth in the sickle, *because the harvest is come"* (verses 28-29).

What God does hold you responsible for knowing is when your harvest has come. Therefore, you have to be expecting it.

For example, when someone tries to hand you a 10 dollar bill, or a 20 dollar bill, just receive it. Don't try to fake being modest and all that — "Oh, no, brother . . . I mean . . . why . . . I just couldn't accept that."

You lying dog. Yes you can. And you know you want to accept it.

Receive it! It's the firstfruits — it's the seed—for your $10,000 and your $20,000.

Take it. Remember, God is trying to get money to you. You are His covenant child and you have no business being buried in debt and having dreams you cannot fulfill.

God Is A Giver

If there is one thing you should know about God and money, it is that God will never hold out on you. That's not His nature. In fact, your heavenly Father is disposed to give to you. Hebrews 11:6 is pretty frank about it:

"But without faith it is impossible to please him: for he that cometh to God must believe that he is, and that he is a *rewarder of them* that diligently seek him."

Do you see that? God is a rewarder. That means He's a giver. God is your rewarder, and you cannot seek Him without getting the reward. One way or another, He is going to give to you. Just look at the pattern throughout Scripture:

John 3:16 "For God so loved the world, that he *gave* his only begotten Son. . . . "

Ephesians 2:8-9 "For by grace are ye saved through faith; and that not of yourselves: it is the *gift* of God."

Matthew 6:33 "Seek ye first the kingdom of God, and his righteousness; and all these things shall be *added* unto you."

Romans 8:32 "He that spared not his own Son, but delivered him up for us all, how shall he not with him also freely *give* us all things?"

Luke 11:13 "If ye then, being evil, know how to give good gifts unto your

children: how much more shall your heavenly Father *give* the Holy Spirit to them that ask him?"

> **"According as his divine power hath *given* unto us all things that pertain unto life and godliness, through the knowledge of him that hath called us to glory and virtue." (2 Peter 1:3)**

God promised you His Son, and He gave. God promised you His Holy Spirit, and He gave. God is willing to give you everything. . . just as He promised. He is not holding anything back.

God is a giver. But if you do not see Him as a giver and understand Him as a giver, you will never walk in the fullness of what He wants you to have — and with God, there are no limits.

So, the real question is this: Are you a receiver?

Are you willing to let yourself, the devil, or someone else, talk you out of this revelation — as well as the wealth — God wants you to have?

God Needs You Rich

Whatever you're trusting God for . . . if you're believing Him for something He has said is yours . . . then who could possibly stop *Him* from giving it to you?

My friend, there are many people — many people, in fact, who love God — who will never receive or understand the message of this book.

Many church people will never allow themselves the opportunity to hear it.

God especially needs you to walk in the fullness of your covenant blessings. He needs you to be wealthy.

Yet, because you have chosen to read this book, God especially needs you to walk in the fullness of your covenant blessings. He needs you to be wealthy.

Why?

In part, He needs you to help make up for those in the Body of Christ who cannot conceive in their wildest imagination that their finances are for reasons bigger than a big house and a big car.

Deuteronomy 8:18, however, is the greatest reason God doesn't want you broke another day in your life. Your financial stability is particularly valuable to God. And here's why:

"But thou shalt remember the Lord thy God: for it is he that giveth thee power to get wealth, that he may *establish his covenant* which he sware unto thy fathers, as it is this day."

It is through your being financially free that God can establish His covenant in the earth. That's right. As one Bible translation puts it, He can establish His covenant through "[your] ability to get wealth or [your] ability to produce wealth."

In other words, you are God's banker in this natural realm. Whatever aspect of the gospel or vision He needs to get over to people, He is looking to you for it.

Since God cannot do anything in the earth without you, He certainly cannot afford for you to be broke. He cannot afford for you to be living from paycheck to paycheck. He cannot even afford for you to be praying under pressure — "How am I going to pay for this, Lord? How am I going to pay for that?"

No. God needs you asking Him, "Where do you want me sow this money, Father?

Who needs this money, Lord? Where does it need to go?"

God didn't tell Abraham, "Look, I've blessed you, now go on about your business. . . . "

No. The heart of God's covenant with Abraham was this:

The bottom line is, if you do not adhere to the wealth message of the gospel, then it will hinder God's work in the earth.

"I'm about to empower you to prosper so much that you will become a blessing to every nation and tribe of people on the face of this earth."

The bottom line is, if you do not adhere to the wealth message of the gospel, then it will hinder God's work in the earth. Satan knows that, which is why he does everything possible to hinder it.

Yes, God is a rewarder. He is a giver . . .

So shalt thou find favour and good understanding in the sight of God and man. Trust in the LORD with all thine heart; and lean not unto thine own understanding. In all thy ways acknowledge him, and he shall direct thy paths.

Be not wise in thine own eyes: fear the LORD, and depart from evil. It shall be health to thy navel, and marrow to thy bones. Honour the LORD with thy substance, and with the first-fruits of all thine increase: So shall thy barns be filled with plenty, and thy presses shall burst out with new wine (Proverbs 3:4-10).

But you are not to be broke another day in your life so God can establish His covenant . . .

Commit thy way unto the Lord; trust also in him; and he shall bring it to pass. And he shall bring forth thy righteousness as the light, and thy judgment as the noonday. Rest in the Lord, and wait patiently for him: fret not thyself because of him who prospereth in his way, because of the man who bringeth wicked devices to pass. Cease from anger, and forsake wrath: fret not thyself in any wise

to do evil. For evildoers shall be cut off:
but those that wait upon the Lord, they
shall inherit the earth (Psalm 37:5-9).

Your ultimate inheritance is the nations. . . the peoples of the earth.

Sadly, however, many church folks are so "spiritually deep" that the work of the Lord almost goes under because they are simply not available to support it.

Don't be like that. Open up your spirit to receive His revelation, and to receive the vast wealth He has for you.

No More Limits

There has been a lot of "hot" discussion about the thirty-fold, sixty-fold and hundredfold harvest in the Body of Christ.

Is it for today? Does it apply to finances?

At the heart of these heated debates is Mark 4:20 — "And these are they which are sown on good ground; such as hear the word, and receive it, and bring forth fruit, some thirty fold, some sixty, and some an hundred."

My friend, I'm here to tell you that our God is interested in something far greater than 30-fold, 60-fold or 100-fold when it comes to your finances.

In fact, I can show you scripture on the thousand fold harvest — "The LORD God of your fathers make you a thousand times so many more as ye are, and bless you, as he hath promised you" (Deuteronomy 1:11). Let that stretch your thinking for a moment.

But now, here's the truth on the whole matter, whether it's 30, 60, 100, or 1,000.

God is limited to blessing your life to the capacity that you are able to receive.

In other words, the only limit God has in your life is the limit of your own capacity to receive.

Only *you* can limit what you can receive from God. God doesn't place any limits on it.

God is not a thirty-fold God. He's not a sixty-fold God. He's not a hundredfold, or even a thousand fold, God.

God is the unlimited God! He is the Most High!

If you will receive that, He will get you to a place where your cup runneth over, to where you cannot count the return on your sowing and giving. You won't be able to figure it, calculate it or -fold it. After all, He's God!

Only God can get you to a place of receiving good measure, pressed down, shaken together, running over (Luke 6:38). A place of receiving "exceeding abundantly above all that we ask or think" (Ephesians 3:30).

What you must do then is work toward increasing your capacity to receive. Don't be just a thirty fold receiver, or a thousand fold receiver. Stop talking about what you cannot have.

When you see something you like, and you cannot have it now, speak to it: "I'll be back for you, yes, sir! In the name of Jehovah Jireh, my Provider, you belong to me. I'll be back, and I won't be long!"

When you release those kinds of faith-filled words into the atmosphere, angels respond. They attend to your prosperity.

This was made so real to me one time in Muncie, Indiana.

As I was preaching, I left my Bible up on the pulpit and I stepped down to the floor. As I remembered my Bible, I looked back to go up the steps and I saw what I thought was a man standing in the pulpit behind my Bible. I particularly noticed his suit. It was brown, with gold spots in it. I liked it. I have three tailors, but I had never seen a suit as nice as that.

Then, suddenly, it irked me that this guy had out dressed me. I was that impressed with his clothes.

Well, I only looked at this guy for a moment, then I turned back to the congregation and I continued to preach.

A moment later, when I looked back to the pulpit, the guy was gone. It didn't take me long to figure out that no one else had seen him. Only I had.

When I got back up to the pulpit, I asked the Lord, "Who was that guy?"

The angel of prosperity, He said. *I send him everywhere you go to back up the message I've told you to preach. I have a host of angels whose only job is to bring prosperity to My people.*

The psalmist boldly declares, "This is the Lord's doing; it is marvelous in our eyes. This is the day which the Lord hath made; we will rejoice and be glad in it. Save now, I beseech thee, O Lord: O Lord, I beseech thee, *send now prosperity*" (Psalm 118:23-25).

Send *now* prosperity!

Luke 19 recounts a very telling story of a short rich man who wanted to see Jesus. Zacchaeus was his name. He was a chief tax collector, and he was very rich.

One day Zacchaeus heard that Jesus was coming through town. So, laying aside his dignity, he climbed a sycamore tree so he could see this Teacher. As Jesus passed by He looked up and saw the man in the tree.

"Zacchaeus," He said to the rich man, "come down. I'm coming over to your place, today."

Now, preachers often talk about this rich man and how attached he was to his money. But I want you to see something else that's very important.

When Zacchaeus was touched by Jesus, the first thing he wanted to make right was the shady business deals that had made him a lot of money. He told Jesus that if he had held back or done anyone wrong, he wanted to return it fourfold. Then he said he wanted to bless the poor. Those were the first things on this rich man's agenda, because when you are truly converted, truly saved, your money is too.

But why did Zacchaeus start talking about money the moment he got into the presence of God?

Romans 1:16 tells us, "For I am not ashamed of the gospel of Christ: *for it is the power of God unto salvation* [*prosperity*] to every one that believeth; to the Jew first, and also to the Greek."

When a person gets saved, prosperity comes with it. Or, as the Spirit of God once told me, *The seed of wealth is on the inside of you waiting to have intercourse with your faith, to bring the manifestation in your life of wealth and prosperity and success.*

That seed of wealth is just waiting to mix with your faith to bring the manifestation of your covenant into your life and into the lives of countless numbers of people around the world.

Yes, prosperity is yours. It is biblically and rightfully yours. But with that prosperity comes a divine purpose. I call it money with a mission. Your money comes from God and it comes with an assignment.

You're Wearing The Blessing

3 chapter

You're Wearing The Blessing

Suppose you had a garment hanging in your closet that you could put on and it would make you *super*. You know, one like Clark Kent had. At the first sign of trouble you duck into the phone booth a wimpy weakling. But you shed your everyday clothes and come out *Superman!*

Within seconds you're transformed into a completely different person—someone who can leap tall buildings in a single bound!

Well, believe it or not, there is such a garment. It's called the *blessing*.

It took me a while to understand this revelation that I'm about to share with you concerning the *blessing*. When I first heard it I knew that it was the truth, yet, I could not fully comprehend it. My mind and my brain had so many of the wrong grooves carved in them.

Besides that, the Body of Christ hasn't been much help where this *blessing* is concerned. Traditionally, the Church has either ignored or side-stepped the fact that our covenant with God empowers us to prosper and be victorious in this lifetime, not just when we get to heaven.

Consequently, the Church has a lot of rethinking to do over this matter of the *blessing*.

Think Singular

To me, the word *blessing*, or *blessed*, had always meant "things" or "events." It was whatever items or good that transpired in my life. It was material gain or tangible substance.

But as you're about to see, God's blessing on your life is not the good things He does for you or gives to you. In reality, the blessing of God is more like a cloak. It's like something you *wear*, not something you *get*.

From the dawn of creation, Adam knew what it was to wear the blessing. He wore it from the moment he took his first breath until he disobeyed God and ate from the tree of the knowledge of good and evil. He knew what it was to have complete dominion and authority over all the earth. Everything was under his control and he enjoyed the goodness of all creation because God had placed the blessing upon him.

A good illustration to help us understand the differences between the *blessing* and the *blessings* is, wind.

When you walk outside and you see children flying kites. . . flags standing straight out from their poles. . . leaves and debris blowing around on the ground. . . you say, "Boy, the wind sure is strong today." Yes, the wind is blowing strong, but what you're really seeing are some of the effects of the wind.

The wind is like the *blessing* and the effects of the wind that you see are like the *blessings*.

Proverbs 10:22 says, "The *blessing* of the Lord, it maketh rich. . . . "

In Galatians 3:14 we read, "That the *blessing* of Abraham might come on the Gentiles through Jesus Christ. . . . "

Notice that both references to *the blessing* are singular in form, not plural. That's telling you the blessing of God is a root to your life. It is not the fruit.

Once you understand that you have *the blessing,* and that you can wear the blessing as though it were a garment, then everything else will be easy. You will no longer be someone trying to get blessed by praying, or by reading a lot of scriptures, or by saying the right confessions.

The blessing is yours. You already have it. And you are guaranteed all the *blessings* that accompany it.

So, when you think *blessing*, start thinking singular.

Dressed to Bless

When God called Abraham apart to establish a covenant with him, He told him, "Get thee out of thy country, and from thy kindred, and from thy father's house, unto a land that I will shew thee: And I will make of thee a great nation, and I will bless thee, and make thy name great; and thou shalt be a blessing: And I will bless them that bless thee, and curse him that curseth thee: and in thee shall all families of the earth be blessed" (Genesis 12:1-3).

In speaking those words to Abraham, God was actually placing the blessing upon him. And with that *blessing* came many *blessings*. Notice what some of those blessings included.

First, God was promising Abraham that His favor would be upon him. He would increase Abraham.

Remember what we saw in Proverbs 10:22?

"The blessing of the Lord, *it maketh rich*, and he addeth no sorrow with it."

When you wear the blessing it makes you rich. It causes things to happen for your good. When you wear the blessing, you cannot stay broke. You cannot stay sick. You cannot stay down or defeated. Why? Because the blessing of the Lord accompanies you everywhere you go.

Psalm 1 describes the covenant man of God as "a tree planted by the rivers of water, that bringeth forth his fruit in his season; his leaf also shall not wither; and *whatsoever he doeth shall prosper*" (verse 3). Everything he touches prospers. It cannot but prosper—because he bears the blessing.

When the Lord pronounces His blessing upon you, and you start walking around with His favor on you—people, situations and things, will not be able to help themselves. They will want to be with you. Because everywhere you go, the blessing goes. And everything good comes from that blessing.

Second, in establishing covenant with Abraham and placing His blessing upon him, God promised, "I will bless them that bless thee, and curse him that curseth thee: and in thee shall all families of the earth be blessed" (Genesis 12:3).

In effect, God was saying, "I will reverse every curse, every idle word, every trap — any evil thing — that anyone tries to do against you."

In Isaiah 54:15 and 17, God's covenant of promise says, "Whosoever shall gather together against thee shall fall for thy sake. . . . No weapon that is formed against thee shall prosper; and every tongue that shall rise against thee in judgment thou shalt condemn."

God is not about to let anyone mess with your blessing. As long as you wear the blessing, no curse can attach itself to you because the curse cannot remain in the presence of, or in the same place as, the blessing.

That's not to say, however, you won't have to remind yourself — and the devil — from time to time. . .

Hey, I don't wear the curse. . . I wear the blessing. And I cannot be cursed.

The point is, you have to wear the blessing in your mind. You have to get it in your head that your God is BIG—and He's big NOW, not just when we all get to heaven.

Finally, the end result of God's placing His blessing upon Abraham was that he would *become a blessing.*

God told Abraham, "And thou shalt be a blessing. . . and in thee shall all families of the earth be blessed" (Genesis 12:2-3).

This matter of being a blessing to other people started with Abraham's own family.

God didn't call Abraham's nephew, Lot, out from among the family. But we see that Lot went anyway. He knew a good deal when he saw one.

Lot prospered greatly by tagging along with his uncle. In fact, Genesis 13 tells us that, in the end, there wasn't enough room for Abraham and Lot to stay together in the same city. Both of them had amassed so much wealth and possessions that they had to split up.

Think about that. As you go through life knowing that you are wearing the blessing, you will have the realization: *Hey, I'm the blessing going somewhere to happen!*

As I said earlier, when you start walking around with the blessing on you to that degree, people will know it. They will notice it. They will be drawn to you. And they will prosper because of you.

Location, Location, Location

There are two great Old Testament examples I want us to examine in order for us to gain insight and understanding into the benefits — as well as the responsibilities — of wearing this *blessing*. The first of these that we will study is Isaac.

In Genesis 26 we're told that a great famine hit the land where Isaac was living. People were leaving left and right to find a better place to live. But not Isaac. God told Isaac, "Go not down into Egypt; dwell in the land which I shall tell thee of: Sojourn in this land, and I will be with thee, and will bless thee. . ." (verses 2-3).

Now why would God tell Isaac to remain in a land ravaged by famine?

The blessing. Isaac was wearing the blessing. There was no need for him to go somewhere else.

He had everything he could possibly need, because he had the blessing.

You see, God is saying, *I just need someone to let me in their neighborhood. I just need someone to let me in their town. All I need is someone to wear this blessing, someone who will listen to Me and obey Me, someone through whom I can bless all families of the earth.*

I tell people all the time how my great-great grandfather was a slave on the sugar cane fields where the church God planted through me now grows. That church is on a old plantation sugar cane field where, today, free people—black, white, red, yellow, brown—come to this crossroads in the middle of nowhere to worship God.

No one but Almighty God could do something like that.

Maybe you're in a land of famine, a place of lack, like Isaac was.

But notice in the end what happened to Isaac:

"Then Isaac sowed in that land, and received in the same year an hundredfold: and the Lord blessed him" (Genesis 26:12).

When everyone else was leaving, Isaac stayed. When everyone else did nothing, Isaac sowed. He trusted God. He obeyed God.

Why? Because he knew he was wearing the blessing. And because of that blessing, Isaac reaped a hundredfold harvest that same year. . . in a land of famine. That's the *blessing*.

New Look. . . New Lifestyle

The moment you decide to take up your blessing and wear the blessing, your life will never be ordinary again.

Take the prophet Elijah, for instance. His life was far from ordinary during a time of serious drought.

During those hard times, 1 Kings 17 tells us that God told Elijah to "hide thyself by the brook

Cherith, that is before Jordan. And it shall be, that thou shalt drink of the brook; and I have commanded the ravens to feed thee there. So he went and did according unto the word of the Lord" (verses 3-5).

For the benefit of those who know they are walking in the blessing, God issues commands to people and situations. And He doesn't always choose to do it in what we would call a "normal" route.

In this case, God used ravens to feed His covenant man.

I remember years ago pastoring a church of about 40 members, half of which were children, in Darrow, Louisiana. During that time I had the opportunity to minister at a much larger church where there were many highly educated people. The Lord ministered powerfully through me there, and I was just certain that it would only be a matter of time before God would say, *OK, pack up and move there. . . that's where I want you now.* But, He never did.

Instead, God chose to use me to touch the world, right there in the tiny cross-roads town of Darrow. Had I been anywhere else, I would have missed God, and I would have missed out on all He has done with me since then.

I stayed where the brook was, where the ravens would come by and feed me.

Now, when you obey God like that, you place yourself in a situation where people will laugh at you, make fun of you, persecute you. Nonetheless, you must be willing to obey the Lord and be faithful—even when He tells you to do something that just by-passes all your natural senses, and your natural ways of thinking.

Everything worked in Elijah's favor as God had said it would. The brook provided water to drink, and the ravens brought bread and meat for him to eat twice a day.

Then, one day the brook dried up. But even faced with a dry brook, he still had the blessing on him. So, God was obligated to move on Elijah's behalf.

"Arise, get thee to Zarephath. . . and dwell there," the Lord told Elijah. "Behold, I have commanded a widow woman there to sustain thee. So he arose and went to Zarephath. And when he came to the gate of the city, behold, the widow woman was there gathering of sticks: and he called to her, and said, Fetch me, I pray thee, a little water in a vessel, that I may drink" (verses 9-10).

Again, God was *commanding* people and situations for Elijah's benefit. But notice, Elijah would never had known the benefit of all God had commanded for his well-being had he not had a willing and obedient heart toward God.

Meanwhile, this was a great opportunity for Elijah to be persecuted by the local people. After all, here's this preacher going to "live off" a poor, starving widow woman and her son. It's bad enough that he's asking for water in the middle of a devastating drought, but in verse 11, he asks for the woman's last bit of food.

The truth is, Elijah didn't ask for her last bit of food. He asked her for the first portion.

"And she said, As the Lord thy God liveth, I have not a cake, but an handful of meal in a barrel, and a little oil in a cruse: and, behold, I am gathering two sticks, that I may go in and dress it for me and my son, that we may eat it, and die. And Elijah said unto her, Fear not; go and do as thou hast said: but make me thereof a little cake first, and bring it unto me, and after make for thee and for thy son" (verses 12-13).

Right here is where the pressure gets real intense.

If the widow had prepared the last little bit of cake for her and her son to eat, she would have eaten her seed, the only seed she had to sow toward her miracle—hers and the prophet's.

Why did Elijah want that first little cake? Because the first one was going to cause the second one. . . and the third one. . . and so on. He wanted it because the *blessing* would be on that first one.

You can be certain that when the man of God takes the first bite because God had instructed him to do so, everything else is going to start multiplying. The supernatural is about to take over.

Sometimes, however, we don't let the supernatural take over because we don't take that important step of obedience. We're busy figuring it out — calculating, equating, educating, acknowledging, but only out of our limited natural abilities.

As the widow woman chose to remain willing and obedient, just as the prophet himself had been, the Word of the Lord came to her:

"For thus saith the Lord God of Israel, The barrel of meal shall not waste, neither shall the cruse of oil fail, until the day that the Lord sendeth rain upon the earth. And she went and did according to the saying of Elijah: and she, and he, and her house, did eat many days. And the barrel of meal wasted not, neither did the cruse of oil fail, according to the word of the Lord, which he spake by Elijah" (verses 14-16).

By hearing that Word from God, faith was able to rise up within the woman and it replaced any fear she might have had. And her faith opened the door for the blessing to manifest in the fullness of blessings. She and her son and the prophet ate many days because the blessing had been released in her house. And the blessing had been released because of her obedience.

The Blessing Is No Put On

So, why is it that so many members of the Body of Christ today are walking around without their *blessing* garment on?

I think the primary reason is that we have not qualified ourselves yet.

Yes, we're saved. Yes, we're filled with the Holy Spirit. Yes, we love the Lord with all our hearts. But are we really ready to handle that kind of blessing God has been talking about all this time?

You see, God has to know that your heart, your soul and your body are all really turned over to Him.

You see, God has to know that your heart, your soul and your body are all really turned over to Him. When He knows that He has *all* of you, then He can release the unlimited effects of the *blessing* on your life.

When it comes down to it, I believe there are a handful of qualities in a believer that mark him or her as capable of wearing the blessing. Those qualities are wisdom, understanding, faithfulness, willingness and obedience—the greatest of these being wisdom and understanding.

When the Lord gave Solomon the chance to ask Him for anything he wanted, Solomon asked for wisdom. And, certainly, God granted Solomon his request, because he remains to this day on biblical record as the wisest man ever to walk this earth, apart from Jesus.

It's no surprise, then, that it was Solomon who wrote:

"Wisdom is the principle thing; therefore get wisdom. . . " (Proverbs 4:7).

It's recorded in 1 Kings 10 that the queen of Sheba once visited Solomon. While he was busy giving her the tour and handing out nuggets of wisdom, the queen was busy looking around at all his *stuff*.

She saw the splendid palace he had built. She saw his fine apparel—even how well his servants were dressed. She saw it all and took note. After all, she was a rich woman herself, but she had nowhere near the wealth, or the wisdom of God, as Solomon.

The reason wisdom is so vitally important to the believer who walks in the blessings of wealth and prosperity is because, in Solomon's own words,

"The prosperity of the fools shall destroy them" (Proverbs 1:32).

In other words, prosperity can only make things worse for someone who is not wise. If you do a little wrong with just a little money, you will only do *big* wrong with plenty of money.

Now, as valuable as wisdom is where the blessing is concerned, understanding is just as important. For, when Solomon declared wisdom to be the "principle thing," he closed that verse by saying, "And with all thy getting get understanding" (Proverbs 4:7).

True understanding is a matter of constantly seeking God's face for insight into every situation.

"Lord, what do you want me to do about this over here. . . How do you want me to handle that over there?"

Proverbs 3:5-6 tells us to "lean not unto thine own understanding. In all thy ways acknowledge him, and he shall direct thy paths."

When you wear the blessing you cannot go by how *you* see situations and circumstances. Rather, it's all about how God sees them.

So, each of these qualities that we have discussed — wisdom, understanding, willingness, faithfulness, obedience — has something to do with the blessing. Because while the blessing leads to the *blessings,* you cannot allow the enjoyment of God's favor on your life to take the place of your walk with Him.

> Because while the blessing leads to the blessings, you cannot allow the enjoyment of God's favor on your life to take the place of your walk with Him.

Apart from all that, however, the Body of Christ still has no concept of how much greater than Abraham, Isaac, Elijah and Solomon, we can — and should be walking in this *blessing.* The covenant under which they lived and ministered comes nowhere close to what is available through our blood-bought covenant.

Sadly enough, we've been struggling as someone without a covenant. Instead of enjoying the stability and full measure of all that rightfully belongs to us, we've lived by the world's ups and downs.

Like Abraham, Isaac and all the others, you live in a land under the threat of lack. . . financial turmoil.

Face it. In this crazy world, there will always be opportunity for something to go wrong, something to blow your mind if you don't know that you are wearing the blessing. When the big scare over Y2K—the rush to be Year 2000 compliant—hit the headlines, people went crazy over it and fear gripped a major portion of the world. Those things will happen.

Nonetheless, they don't have to affect you. Not while you're wearing the blessing.

So, put on your *blessing*. Make up your mind and then declare boldly. . .

Galatians 3:13-14 says, "Christ hath redeemed [me] from the curse of the law. . . that the blessing of Abraham might come on [me]. . . . " Therefore,

I purpose to put on the blessing—and that blessing makes everything else happen.

It doesn't matter what my last name is. It doesn't matter which part of town I come from. It doesn't matter what color my skin is, or how much education I do or don't have. I'm a child of God and His blessing has been pronounced upon me.

What's more, Ephesians 1:3 says my Heavenly Father "hath [has already] blessed [me] with all spiritual blessings in heavenly places in Christ." So, it is settled. I have it NOW! I have the blessing NOW!

My brother or sister, once you step over into that realm of always wearing *your* blessing, nothing will ever stop you. Not recession. Not famine. Not people's comments against you. Nothing.

And when you reach that point, you will never be broke another day in your life because *blessings* will be chasing you down.

Passing The Money Test

4 chapter

Passing The Money Test

If you were to get a concept of the kind of money God really wants you to have, it would amaze you. Because when the *Most High God* starts talking about wealth and riches, it can overload the human mind.

After all, our God is an "exceeding abundantly above all that we ask or think" kind of God (Ephesians 3:20). And as we've seen up to this point, we are the object of His blessing.

It's no secret, however, that money and riches — the blessings that our Father wants to pour out on us—carry with them a certain power, political power, social power and the like. But while money is neither evil nor righteous in itself, it does take upon itself the personality or spirit of the person who has it.

Therefore, if you are not totally committed to righteousness, you will do wrong things with money. And in the end, that money will destroy you.

When I first began teaching the revelations I had received from the Lord concerning financial prosperity, I would look across congregations and I could tell that most of the people simply were not ready for wealth and riches—the kind that their God had in mind for them. If they had gotten their hands on large amounts of money, it would have wiped them out. It would have been no different than the stories you hear about people winning the lottery and in a year being broke again, or more in debt than they ever imagined.

Besides that, as I looked at these "people of the covenant"—the covenant that guaranteed all this wealth and prosperity — I wondered what was keeping them from receiving what was rightfully theirs.

If tithing were all that was necessary to qualify them for these blessings, I figured most people in the church would be pretty well set.

If holiness were all that was necessary to qualify, why did a holy man of God, a prophet who had walked with Elisha (2 Kings 4), die and leave his wife in such debt that the creditors were going to take their children and force them into slavery?

My friend, it's time for the Church to learn now how to handle money and get on with God's plan so we can advance to the next level. . . and to the next. . . and the next.

Can You Handle Being Rich?

There are two spectrums of money's power.

First, there is the power to get money. We saw that in Deuteronomy 8:18—"But thou shalt remember the Lord thy God: for it is he that giveth thee power to get wealth. . . . "

But, then, there is the power to handle money. The power to keep it.

According to Ephesians 3:20, the power to handle wealth and money is that anointing of God that is already resident within us:

"Now unto him that is able to do exceeding abundantly above all that we ask or think, according to the *power that worketh in us.* . . . "

As a born-again believer, you need the power of God — His anointing — constantly at work within you. For it is by His Spirit and the revelation of His Word that you handle the wealth and riches He permits you to steward, or manage. What you need, however, is to be developed in how to apply that power as a money manager.

In Luke 16:1-13, Jesus taught His disciples the parable of the unrighteous steward, and in the first two verses we learn that the steward was caught wasting his master's goods. "Give an account of thy stewardship," his master told him, "for thou mayest be no longer steward" (verse 2).

Being a good steward, being a good money manager, does not mean buying cheap toilet paper and turning out the lights all the time, though we all have a responsibility to not be wasteful.

Even Jesus, in the middle of the miracle of feeding thousands of people with a little boy's loaves and fishes, told His disciples, "Gather up the fragments that remain, *that nothing be lost*" (John 6:12). The Lord was not wasteful.

I believe many are financially broke simply because they are wasteful with what they already have. They're not gathering up the fragments which could amount to a lot. Many of them have a lot of things lying around that they could turn into money and at least use as seed to sow for an even greater harvest.

But, now, notice what the master in this parable told his manager — "Thou mayest be no longer steward."

Some people in the Church may think they're one of God's stewards, but they're really not. Actually, they're like this guy trying to "make it" on his own.

How about you? Do you really consider your job as your only hope?

If it is, no real supernatural anointing will ever manifest in your life, or your circumstances.

I believe a large part of the Church has been temporarily put out of stewardship because God cannot trust them to take care of His business. They're not tithing. They're not giving offerings. They're not taking care of their men and women of God—their ministers of the gospel—as they should.

Who wants a thief for a manager? God certainly doesn't.

So, once the steward's wastefulness was exposed, and it was obvious that he was fired, he did something interesting. He started "working the system" — the unrighteous system, that is. He used his position and his boss's money to secure his future as best as he could by making "friends" for himself.

A good sinner is crooked and knows how to work the system. He connives his way to the top, and even gains respect for it. In fact, the unrighteous steward's master ended up commending him for being so crafty in what he did, to which Jesus commented:

"For the children of this world are in their generation wiser than the children of light" (verse 8).

The bottom line is, the world does a far better job working their system than we do ours.

Jesus ended this parable by saying, "No servant can serve two masters: for either he will hate the one, and love the other; or else he will hold to the one, and despise the other. Ye cannot serve God and mammon [money]" (Luke 16:13).

For too long much of the Church has had the wrong idea about money because they have misinterpreted this verse. Yes, it is saying that no man can serve two masters. But what people have heard in their religious minds is, *God's telling me to leave this money thing alone.*

That's not so. God is not telling you to keep your hands off money. We've already established that wealth and riches are yours by covenant right. What God is telling you to do is to take authority over it. Take authority over your money. Because, if you do not lord over your money, it will certainly lord over you.

Jesus' point in telling His disciples this parable about the unrighteous steward was to challenge them to manage wisely what they already had. In Luke 16:10-11, He added, "He that is faithful in that which is least is faithful also in much. If therefore ye have not been faithful in that unrighteous mammon, who will commit to your trust the true riches?"

In other words, take the money test. God will check you out with the *least* before He advances you to *more*. That means anyone can qualify—right where you are in life. Just be willing to become more faithful with what you have now. Be quick to do what God tells you to do with it. Don't let it control you. You control it.

Money's Danger Zones

How many times have you heard this verse quoted?

"Money is the root of all evil. . . " — 1 Timothy 6:10.

However many times you've heard it quoted like that, that's the number of times you've heard it *misquoted*.

It doesn't say *money* is the root of all evil, it says the *love of money* is the root of all evil.

Remember, money in itself is neither evil nor righteous. It's your attitude and behavior concerning money that either brings righteousness or evil onto the scene. That means you could have all the money in the world and still walk righteous and blameless in God's eyes.

To reach that point, however, there are some danger zones you need to avoid. . . other money tests you will have to pass. That's where we give heed to the Apostle Paul's warning in 1 Timothy 6:17-18: "Charge them that are rich in this world, that they be not highminded, nor trust in uncertain riches, but in the living God, who giveth us richly all things to enjoy; That they do good, that they be rich in good works, ready to distribute, willing to communicate."

Yes, God "giveth us richly all things to enjoy." To enjoy those things, however, there are conditions.

First, Paul says to "be not highminded."

Did you know you can be broke and still be high-minded?

Check yourself.

Are you able to handle correction well? How about from your pastor? Or, your boss at work? Do you go behind their backs and gossip about them or put them down?

Better, yet. How about people who are a little better off than you—a bigger house, a newer car, nicer clothes? If you see someone who is blessed and you have a hard time with what they have, that's a good indication that you are high-minded.

The Apostle Peter said, "Humble yourselves therefore under the mighty hand of God, that he may exalt you in due time" (1 Peter 5:6).

That should be encouraging because, again, you can start by humbling yourself where you are right now. Just ask the Lord to help you walk in humility, and you will pass the test.

A second danger zone to avoid is trusting in uncertain riches.

As a pastor, I'm not stupid. I know a lot of church people would stop praying, reading their Bibles and coming to church, if they had more money and less lack.

"Yeah, but, you see, Reverend, I've got me a fine 22-foot boat parked down at the marina. And if I don't skip church today. . . well, when am I ever going to get to enjoy it?"

It's that "stuff" that will call you away from God unless you use it for God.

Oh, yes, get yourself the biggest boat down at the marina, but glorify God in it. Let people see and hear you glorify God over the things you have received from Him. Let them know that God is a good God, and that it was He who got those things for you. That's how you can use your blessings for Him.

The real test here is, if you are not properly han-dling what you have right now — you're not hearing

God and doing what He tells you to do with your money—then you are trusting in uncertain riches.

If you don't trust God enough to do what He tells you to do with what you have, then you are actually saying, "God, I trust the money I have in the bank more than I trust you."

In reality, it's the people who don't have a lot of money that tend to trust in uncertain riches. They're more fearful about releasing what little money they do have. Consequently, fear is one of the greatest enemies of stewardship.

Instead of trusting in uncertain riches, Paul said to trust in the living God. As you do, you will find yourself agreeing with David when he said:

"O taste and see that the Lord is good: blessed is the man that *trusteth* in him. O fear the Lord, ye his saints: for there is *no want* to them that fear him. The young lions do lack, and suffer hunger: but they that seek the Lord *shall not want* any good thing" (Psalm 34:8-10).

Remember these covenant promises. . .

God gives you power to gain wealth

> (Deuteronomy 8:18).

God wants you to have every good and perfect gift

> (James 1:17).

God is your Shepherd and you shall not want

> (Psalms 23:1).

God will supply all your needs according to His riches in glory by Christ Jesus

> (Philippians 4:19).

Two Sides to Receiving

Finally, another money test for you to pass is your being "ready to distribute, willing to communicate" (1 Timothy 6:18).

God is glad to give to you richly, or plentifully — in abundance — for you to enjoy. But then He also expects you to be rich in good works, too. That means ready to distribute, willing to communicate. I call it the "spiritual law of exchange."

This exchange is seen in Jesus' promise to us in Luke 6:38:

"Give, and it shall be given unto you; good measure, pressed down, and shaken together, and running over, shall men give into your bosom. For with the same measure that ye mete withal it shall be measured to you again."

That sounds like harvest to me. Sounds like reaping more than you sowed — "good measure, pressed down, and shaken together, and running over."

Now, Christians often jump to Philippians 4:19, which I just listed as a covenant promise — "But my God shall supply all your need according to his riches in glory by Christ Jesus." They start confessing that all their needs are met.

What many of them do not understand, however, is that verse 19 does not work by itself. There was an exchange made *before* the Apostle Paul got to that verse.

Notwithstanding ye have well done, that ye did communicate with my affliction. Now ye Philippians know also, that in the beginning of the gospel, when I departed from Macedonia, no church communicated with me as concerning giving and receiving, but ye only. For even in Thessalonica ye sent once and again unto my necessity. Not because I desire a gift: but I desire fruit that may abound to your account. But I have all, and abound: I am full, having received of Epaphroditus the things which were sent from you, an odour of a sweet smell, a sacrifice acceptable, wellpleasing to God (Philippians 4:14-18).

Notice the word *communicate* in verses 14 and 15. Paul explains that their *communicating* was all about giving — *and* — receiving. It was all about exchange. And in verse 17, Paul shoots real straight with them and says, "Hey, I didn't come to get money, or a gift, *from* you. No, I came to get it *to* you."

The law of exchange says that something will come *to* you as soon as you plant your offering, or your seed. At first, that something is *expectation.* Expectation is what you hold on to until you see a manifestation of your harvest.

Now, on a practical aspect of this spiritual law of exchange, you may want to do something I started doing in the earlier days of my financial deliverance. It was something that helped me hold on to my expectation until I saw a manifestation. I kept a log of my giving.

Every time I gave something to anyone, I recorded it. Then, I would go back and remind God about specific things I had given, and I would ask Him what He was doing about it.

On one side of the book I recorded what I gave, and on the other side I recorded what I received. My returns far surpassed what I had given. Still, I had it there to hold before God, which helped keep my expectations up.

The point is, it's up to you to activate this spiritual law of exchange. And you activate it by giving.

It's up to you to activate this spiritual law of exchange. And you activate it by giving.

You have to work both sides of the system — the giving. . . then receiving, the sowing. . . then reaping — not just try to cash in on part of it, the receiving part. You must deposit into an account from which God can supply "all your need according to his riches in glory by Christ Jesus."

I remember the Lord once telling me to give $100 to a gentleman whom I did not know very well. You need to know that in those days, $100 was like $10,000 to me today. Yet, I knew I had to get it to him because this was God talking.

Well, I went to the man's house to give him the money, but he wasn't there. That was ok, because, suddenly, that didn't seem to matter anymore.

What mattered was. . . his house was bigger than mine!

I said, "Lord! Why do You want me to give him this money? He should be giving me something!"

So, I left and went looking for this guy. I found him at a restaurant. When I went inside, sure enough, there he sat. . . with a huge steak hanging off the edges of his plate.

I thought, *My God, look at this man — he's in here eating a steak!*

Anyway, I told him the Lord had sent me to give him some money, and I gave him the $100. To be honest with you, I had to hurry up and get out of there before I asked him for the money back.

That was the kind of shape I was in back then. And the Lord had to take me through some money tests. He will do the same to you. He does it for all of us.

Just remember, take authority over every dollar you have — whether it's $100, or $10,000. Take your stand of authority and make Jesus the Lord over every dollar you handle. Then listen to Him and obey Him as to what you are to do with it.

Your financial prosperity is no cycle. It's no lucky lottery ticket, either. "I'll never be broke another day in my life!" is not some "wave" passing through the Church. What it is. . . is covenant.

If you have faith for financial abundance, if you have wisdom and understanding, if you are faithful — you will pass the money test. . . and you will step over into a realm of wealth and riches beyond your wildest dreams and imaginations.

Casino or Covenant —
What's Your Ticket Out?

5 chapter

Casino or Covenant — What's Your Ticket Out?

I remember having an eye-opening conversation one time with a nice, young Christian man about his hopes for the future. This is what he had to say:

"I know there's more for me in life. . . and I like nice things. But every now and then, when I don't have enough money, I go to the casino. Sure, I lose sometimes. But I take a chance."

Now, there's a believer who knows little-to-nothing about his covenant.

When he told me this, he looked at me because he knew that I knew—I knew my covenant. He had never seen me at any of those casinos, and yet he knew I had the goods. . . I had all the nice things flowing through my life and ministry. He also knew that I knew some things he didn't know.

What about you? Are you betting on the casino or are you trusting in your covenant to get you out of financial debt and over into abundance?

The owners of those casinos certainly are not richer than God. Sadly, however, whole generations of believers are being raised up to think — and live — just the opposite. Children of God are walking out the church doors and into the world without any hope for a happy and prosperous future.

From Have-Nots to Haves

It hasn't been all that long ago that the Lord said something that really made me mad.

The world has been ruling the church by wealth, He told me. *Sinners have been ruling over Christians by their wealth, and the Church has not taken her rightful place of reigning and ruling.*

Certainly, it's no secret that this problem of God's people not ruling and reigning in the earth as they should have has been around a long time. It started back in the Garden of Eden the moment Adam sinned. Adam was God's man, but through his disobedience, in effect, he handed everything over to the devil — and it's been a nagging problem ever since.

There are only two types of people in this world — the lender and the borrower. We call them the haves and the have nots.

Still, I got angry when the Lord brought all that up, but then He took me to about six passages of scripture, the first of which was Proverbs 22:7. . .

"The rich ruleth over the poor, and the borrower is servant to the lender."

Now, let me give you a real deep revelation about this scripture. There are only two types of people in this world — the lender and the borrower. We call them the *haves* and the *have nots*. The haves rule because they have all the money. The have nots are servants because they don't have any money. In the world system whoever has the money, rules. It's that simple.

In our case, the reason the world has been ruling over the Church all these years is because the world has had all the money, and the Church has had nothing. That's because, over the years, the devil has done a good job of talking us into being real spiritual over our lack — "Yes, we're just poor, humble servants of God. . . and the more poor we get the more anointed we are. . . . "

Consequently, when we needed something, we had to go to the world for it. We had to borrow. We might get some great revelation from God about building something or doing something, but then we have to go to someone else, someone with money, to find out if we can do what God told us to do, or not.

May God forgive us for all the religious excuses we've made up for being broke.

The truth is, if we don't have some wealth — a lot of wealth, to be exact—accompanying that anointing, then we still have nothing. And we will never really rule and reign for God in this earthly realm.

So when the Lord took me to that scripture, it didn't seem very encouraging. But then He showed me the verse just before it, Proverbs 22:6 — "Train up a child in the way he should go: and when he is old, he will not depart from it."

There it was. A divine connection. A key to getting entire generations of Church people out of financial bondage. . .

Training up our children.

You and I can train up our children in finances the same as we can train them up in anything else. We can train them to live by the covenant instead of living by the system of credit. We can train them to go to God as their source for "stuff" instead of to the casino.

In short, you and I have the power to get our generation of believers back on track.

We find a similar situation to this recorded in Nehemiah 5. This was back in the days when the people of Israel were scattered and their beloved Jerusalem lay in ruins.

And there was a great cry of the people. . . We have mortgaged our lands, vineyards, and houses, that we might buy corn, because of the [famine]. There were also that said, We have borrowed money for the king's [taxes], and that upon our lands and vineyards. Yet now our flesh is as the flesh of our brethren, our children as their children: and, lo, we bring into bondage our sons and our daughters to be servants, and some of our daughters are brought unto bondage already: neither is it in our power to

redeem them; for other men have our lands and vineyards (verses 1-5).

This passage of scripture reminds me of that young man whose only real hope for doing any better in life was going to the casino—which is why I'm like Nehemiah:

"I was very angry when I heard their cry and *these words*" (verse 6).

What were their words?

We're broke! We're in debt! Everything we have — including our children — is mortgaged!

You'll notice that verse 3 says they were also in a time of famine.

These covenant people of God were like that casino-hopping man. They had no knowledge or understanding of their covenant. If they had, they would have done like their covenant fathers before them — Abraham, Isaac, Joseph — and sailed right through that famine untouched. In fact, they probably would have even come out ahead. . . with a profit.

This passage points to the same kind of financial slavery that we as the Body of Christ face today. The only difference is that we've been convinced by the devil and the world that it's normal to be living this way. That's why the Church has been living under financial bondage for generations.

So, where does that leave us?

If we're ever going to get out of this money rat race, we're going to have to lay hold of the revelation that the Jews in Nehemiah's day received. It says the people cried out and said, "Neither is it in our power to redeem them" (verse 5).

We cannot redeem our sons and daughters. We cannot redeem our houses and lands. Husbands working two jobs, wives working two jobs, single parents working three — it just won't do. Our education, our professional skills, our natural abilities will not cut it.

What a Good Cry Will Do

As we read down through Nehemiah 5, we find that Nehemiah called a great assembly of the haves and the have nots and came up with a God-inspired plan for helping get the people out from under this bondage. In verse 11, we read:

"*Restore,* I pray you, to them, even this day, their lands, their vineyards, their oliveyards, and their houses, also the hundredth part of the money, and of the corn, the wine, and the oil, that ye exact of them."

Restoration is on the way.

You may be thinking, *Yeah, but I've never been rich. How can you restore something you never had in the first place?*

When Jesus died on the cross, He took your debts the same as He took your infirmities, your sorrows, your weaknesses. . . all your sin and all your unrighteousness, once and for all.

Now, notice the response of the haves, or the lenders, to Nehemiah's request on behalf of the have nots in verse 12:

"Then said they, We will *restore* them, and will *require nothing of them;* so will we do as thou

> Restoration is coming to the Body of Christ. We are to be restored to our rightful place, to our rightful possessions.

sayest. Then I [Nehemiah] called the priests, and took an oath of them, that they should do according to this promise."

The children, the land, the houses — everything — was restored to the Jews. And it was done apart from their own ability. Their ways had failed miserably. Only God could have delivered them.

The haves responded to Nehemiah's demands by saying, we will "do as thou sayest."

So someone had to *say* some things. Someone had to do the talking.

Restoration is coming to the Body of Christ. We are to be restored to our rightful place, to our rightful possessions. But that restoration can only come by revelation and by resurrection — that is,

there must be a resurrection anointing of empowerment in individuals who are ready to go forth and
walk in that type of lifestyle.

All along, it has been Satan trying to hold us
back from what is rightfully ours. Yet, we have not
taken the stand that we should. We have allowed
the devil, and the world's system, to intimidate us
and keep us down financially.

Meanwhile, the world is actually afraid of us.
Politicians, the government, and so on, really don't
want to mess with the Church. Because, in reality,
the Church has immeasurable power. It is we who
should be calling the shots, not the world, not even
the world's leaders. But we're too busy yielding to
the world's mess and denying our own power and
rightful place in the earth.

When you come across a scripture like 2 Timothy
3:5 —"Having a form of godliness, but denying the
power thereof. . ." — you have to ask yourself:

*I am denying the power? Or, am I applying the
power?*

Granted, the context of this verse refers to people who are living ungodly lives. Nonetheless, the principle still holds true.

What I'm saying is that the Church has been in denial, and it's no different than alcoholics or addicts denying they have a problem. You'll never get anywhere until you face up to the truth.

The truth is, there are many in the Church who have a "form of prosperity, but deny the power thereof." They look prosperous because they have houses, but they also have mortgages. They look prosperous because they have nice cars, but they've taken out loans. They look prosperous because they have fine furniture, clothes, jewelry, and so on, but they've bought it all on credit.

Now, I will say this: It is not a sin to borrow money. The Bible doesn't call borrowing a sin.

In a practical sense, however, if you borrow money, then make it work for you. Whatever you do with borrowed money should make more interest for you than what you have to pay the lender.

Where our generation has gone wrong is that we've been borrowing money just to live, and that's not normal. It's not right. We've become a servant to the lenders. They are making us pay their bills instead of them paying ours. That is not prosperity. That is not God's best for our lives.

If you want the best, then it's time to break out of that cycle by crying out and acknowledging that you are broke. You need to get off the credit system and get on to God's. Furthermore, it's time to start speaking your deliverance. . .

I'll never be broke another day in my life!

When God Pays the Bills

God wants to activate money miracles for you. And you're not the first person to ever need one. Just read the Bible. It's full of money miracles and financial deliverances that God did for those who would believe Him.

One in particular is found in Matthew 17.

When Peter went to Jesus to tell Him that they owed money for taxes, Jesus mentioned it to Peter first, telling him, "Go thou to the sea, and cast an hook, and take up the fish that first cometh up; and when thou hast opened his mouth, thou shalt find a piece of money: that take, and give unto them for me and thee" (verse 27).

Just as we see God performing a money miracle here, He can and will do the same for you. I know, He has done many for me.

Let me be the first to tell you that I have done some crazy things in my day, buying all kinds of things on credit that I didn't have any business buying. And I cannot tell you how many times in the natural sense, I did not have the power to redeem myself from those seemingly hopeless situations, like the Jews we read about in Nehemiah 5. But I got my heart right, and then God did the rest.

Deuteronomy 28:12 tells us, "The Lord shall open unto thee his *good treasure,* the heaven to give the rain unto thy land in his season, and to bless all the work of thine hand: *and thou shalt lend* unto many nations, *and thou shalt not borrow."*

God is in the business of doing miracles and making ways for you, such that you'll never have to be the borrower again. He can make you the lender. To reach that point,

God is in the business of doing miracles and making ways for you, such that you'll never have to be the borrower again.

however, you must fasten that into your faith and into your spirit with expectation and supernatural hope, just as people like Abraham had to do.

God's method of operation in performing miracles wasn't one way for Abraham, Isaac, Jesus, Peter, and then another way for you. No. The same God Who gave them the ability to call things that be not as though they were is the same God Who is talking to you about your situation, right now.

Abraham so locked on to the covenant promises of God that the Bible says he reached a point where he was fully persuaded that He was able to perform what He had promised (see Romans 4). That's where you need to be. Fully persuaded.

Now, let's look again at a scripture we studied earlier in this book. I want you to see how God's way of delivering out of lack and into abundance compares to the world's way.

> **Deuteronomy 8:17-18 (*The Amplified Bible*):**
>
> **"Beware lest you say in your [mind and] heart, My power and the might of my hand have gotten me this wealth. But you shall (earnestly) remember the Lord your God; for it is He Who gives you power to get wealth, that He may establish His covenant which He swore to your fathers, as at this day."**

This verse is referring to the Hebrew people who God had delivered out of slavery in Egypt and made wealthy by no effort of their own. There was no way they could have gotten rich as a bunch of slaves that had been oppressed for 400 years. If they could have done it on their own, it seems like 400 years would have been enough time to at least have broken even.

But notice how God can get pretty extreme where His people are concerned. He brought them out of bondage loaded down with gold and riches. They were slaves one day and millionaires the next.

The anointing is there. The miracle working power is there. The financial deliverance is there. . . . All the power is just waiting inside you to be activated. How? By your giving.

But only in God's way of doing things. It was His power that did it. It was His power that caused them to gain wealth.

Today, that same power is resident within you and available to move on your behalf at any moment.

You'll remember that Ephesians 3:20 said God is "able to do exceeding abundantly above all that [you] ask or think, according to the power that worketh in [you]."

The anointing is there. The miracle working power is there. The financial deliverance is there.

To be quite frank with you, I cannot even think broke anymore. That's because there's a certain freedom when you step out of lack and into abundance.

And as we saw at the close of the last chapter, all of the power is just waiting inside you to be activated. How? By your giving.

In other words, you have to cooperate with it. And part of that cooperation also involves *asking* and *thinking*.

The Apostle Paul said "above all that [you] *ask* or *think*. . . . " He's saying, first, you need to ask. And some people think that is wrong. But Paul makes the point that God goes beyond what you ask. James 4:2 says that "[you] have not, because [you] ask not."

Lord, would you please deliver me out of this rat race. . . this slavery?

Second, Paul shows where our thinking needs to be — in line with what God thinks. We need our minds renewed. You truly need to think rich.

To be quite frank with you, I cannot even think broke anymore. That's because there's a certain freedom when you step out of lack and into abundance. People and circumstances don't control you, anymore.

So, cooperate with God. Cooperate by your giving. Cooperate by your asking. Cooperate by your thinking.

Jesus asked two blind men who were persistent in asking for their deliverance, "Believe ye that I am able to do this?"

"Yea, Lord," they said (Matthew 9:28).

They cooperated. . . and were healed.

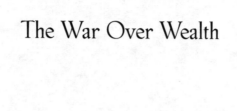

The War Over Wealth

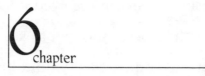

chapter 6

The War Over Wealth

The key to any system of slavery or bondage that we've ever seen on this earth has been ignorance.

Throughout history in which a particular race was enslave by another race, ignorance was a primary tool in keeping the enslaved race in bondage. And by *ignorance* I mean, they were kept from seeing the "outside" world, or the real world.

Had the enslaved person received knowledge of the situation, or had been allowed to see the complete picture of their state, they would have broken out of their shackles much earlier. And while the enslaved race was denied the truth, they were constantly being reprogrammed by the the master to think like a slave, or opposite of who and what they truly were.

In principle, that's the same method of bondage Satan has used against the church for the past few centuries concerning prosperity, gifts of the Spirit, healing, speaking in tongues, and so on. The devil has done whatever was necessary to keep Christians ignorant, blinded, powerless and broke.

In short, we've been at war, and the devil has used everything possible to keep the Body of Christ down and defeated.

He's Going for Your Wallet

In 1994, I received a wonderful prophecy concerning my life and ministry. It was an inspiring and encouraging word from the Lord. But after all the nice words —". . .for I [God] will give you blessing, blessing, blessing. . ."— came this sobering warning:

"And the enemy [Satan] would come in to try to tear it apart, to try and direct it another way. . . . "

Now, why did the devil have to stick his ugly head up right in the middle of my prophecy and mess everything up. . . just when it was sounding so nice and wonderful?

We're at war, that's why. And like it or not, those not so pleasant words spoken to me have come to pass, just the same as the pleasant ones have.

But, now, don't get me wrong. Satan's fight against me is not about Leroy Thompson. No, it's about this gospel I preach. It's about this Word of God that he has been trying to shut down for the past 6,000 years of human history.

Even now, I guarantee you that the devil is trying to do everything he can to stop you from believing a word that I'm saying. Because, if he can shut this Word down — *"I'll never be broke another day in my life!"* — then he can keep you, me and the rest of the Church in financial bondage, which is his final stronghold against the Body of Christ.

You see, even way back in the early days of the Old Testament, Satan was fighting long and hard against this idea of man being blessed by God with wealth and riches.

In the account of Job's testings and trials, it was all about "stuff." The devil was trying to get God's "stuff" away from Job.

"There was a man in the land of Uz, whose name was Job; and that man was perfect and upright, and one that feared God, and eschewed evil. And there were born unto him seven sons and three daughters. His substance also was seven thousand sheep, and three thousand camels, and five hundred yoke of oxen, and five hundred she asses, and a very great household; so that this man was the greatest of all the men of the east" (Job 1:1-3).

First, we're told that Job was a holy man. He walked upright before God. He honored and reverenced God. Now, we can handle that in our religious minds, right?

But, then, look at what happens. We're given this long list of Job's wealth.

Why did God bother to list all of Job's "stuff?" He could have put something else in there for us to read. He shouldn't have put all this carnality in verse three. I mean, look at it all the stuff.

Surely, Job was carnal. Surely, he was greedy and materialistic. . . a money-grubbing. . . flesh-driven kind of man.

No. He was holy. He was upright. What we need to get in our heads is that there is nothing *carnal* about being blessed. In fact, holy and upright people are supposed to have wealth and riches. Just look at verse 3 and see how much they're supposed to have.

Remember Psalms 112:1-3?

"Blessed is the man that feareth the Lord, that delighteth greatly in his commandments. His seed shall be mighty upon earth: the generation of the upright shall be blessed. Wealth and riches shall be in his house: and his righteousness endureth for ever."

Wealth and riches shall be in his house. . .

Sounds like a good description of Job. Wealth and riches belong in the house of the upright.

Well, my brother and sister, I want you to see that it wasn't Job's holiness that made him the greatest among all the men of the east.

It's interesting to note the connection — as far as God is concerned — between righteousness, holiness, uprightness and riches. All of these characteristics of a person who loves and reverences God are associated with wealth and riches.

In contrast, the devil has been trying to get the Church's eyes off the "wealth and riches" part and focused on the "holiness" part—as if the two could never mix.

Well, my brother and sister, I want you to see that it wasn't Job's holiness that made him the greatest among all the men of the east. His holiness played a big part in his becoming "the greatest." But my point is, people in the East didn't go around comparing their holiness to Job's.

No. It was all that "stuff" that got their attention. They took note of his wealth. He was judged "the greatest" because of his material goods.

So, if Satan is at war with the righteous men and women of God, where do you think he is most likely to attack someone like Job — "the greatest of all the men of the east" — who has this impressive train of blessings, a train of material gains that God had put on his life?

Job 1:6-11 gives us the answer:

> **Now there was a day when the sons of
> God came to present themselves before the
> Lord, and Satan came also among them.
> And the Lord said unto Satan, Whence**

comest thou? Then Satan answered the Lord, and said, From going to and fro in the earth, and from walking up and down in it. And the Lord said unto Satan, Hast thou considered my servant Job, that there is none like him in the earth, a perfect and an upright man, one that feareth God, and escheweth evil? Then Satan answered the Lord, and said, Doth Job fear God for nought? Hast not thou made an hedge about him, and about his house, and about all that he hath on every side? thou hast blessed the work of his hands, and his substance is increased in the land. But put forth thine hand now, and touch all that he hath, and he will curse thee to thy face.

The first thing the devil attacked in Job's life was his substance. He wanted Job's "stuff." The first thing God had to say about Job was, *He's my man. . . And did I tell you he was rich. Let me tell*

you how rich he is. . . .

Regaining Enemy Territory

Jesus was no exception to Satan's pattern of all out warfare against wealth and riches.

In Luke 4:5-6, we find the account of Satan's tempting Jesus. Notice the point of his attack.

"And the devil, taking him up into an high mountain, shewed unto him all the kingdoms of the world in a moment of time. And the devil said unto him, All this power will I give thee, and the glory of them: for that is delivered unto me; and to whomsoever I will I give it."

Satan showed Jesus the material kingdoms of the earth — all their wealth, all their riches, all their goods, anything that could possibly represent material power and glory in this natural realm.

In other words, the devil showed Jesus "things" that in some way had to tempt His natural flesh. Otherwise, it would not have been a temptation.

Then, he tells Jesus that all of it was his to give to whomsoever he willed. And that was right. We've already seen how the "first Adam" handed all the authority and dominion over this material world over to Satan the moment he disobeyed God and ate from the tree of the knowledge of good and evil.

But Satan didn't need to bother offering to *give* all the glory of the material world to Jesus. Jesus — the "Second Adam" — was already in the process of *taking* it all back and giving it to the Church. He didn't need the devil's generosity.

Meanwhile, Jesus was about to launch His own attack against the devil in this war over wealth and riches.

Jesus' first assault against lack came in the form of a miracle — His first one recorded — at a wedding feast where the host ran out of wine for the guests and Jesus turned large pots of water into wine. . . exceptionally fine wine, at that (see John 2).

But it was in Luke 4 that Jesus declared all out war against poverty and lack.

"The Spirit of the Lord is upon me," He proclaimed, "because he hath anointed me to preach the gospel to the *poor;* he hath sent me to heal the brokenhearted, to preach deliverance to the captives, and recovering of sight to the blind, to set at liberty them that are bruised. To preach the acceptable year of the Lord [the year when all debt was wiped out]" (Luke 4:18-19).

The very first thing Jesus attacked with that anointing was lack — "because he hath anointed me to preach the gospel to the poor."

What was His "gospel"?

You don't have to be poor anymore. The Anointed One and His anointing has redeemed you from the curse of the law. . . the curse of poverty, the curse of lack, the curse of insufficiency, the curse of barely getting by (Galatians 3:13).

In effect, Jesus was saying, "I am anointed to remove burdens, destroy yokes and pull down strongholds built by Satan."

From 2 Corinthians 10:3-5, we know that a stronghold is anything that opposes God's will, and that the first place you have to attack it is in your mind.

"For though we walk in the flesh, we do not war after the flesh. For the weapons of our warfare are not carnal, but mighty through God to the pulling down of strongholds; casting down imaginations and every high thing that exalteth itself against the knowledge of God, and bringing into captivity every thought to the obedience of Christ."

In the case of this financial stronghold Satan has built against the Church, you can pull out your sword of the Spirit — God's Word — and cut away at the devil's lies from your thinking.

Pull out 3 John 2, which says, "Beloved, I wish above all things that thou mayest *prosper* and *be in health,* even as *thy soul prospereth.*"

This verse in particular shows the priority of material prosperity in a list of three — prospering in goods and finances, prospering in your body with physical health and prospering in your soul. . . your mind, will and emotions. This is a pattern we can find throughout the Bible.

Psalm 105:37 recounts how God brought Israel out of bondage from Egypt "with silver and gold: and there was not one feeble person among their tribes." Again, material wealth is listed first, then physical health.

Time and time again, God saw fit to place material prosperity at the top of these lists, yet, the devil has beaten us down and condemned us to the point that we've put our financial prosperity at the bottom of the list, if we even put it on the list at all.

No, my brother and sister, money is the elementary anointing. God respects it, and so should we.

Besides, why else would God allow a verse such as Psalm 35:27 to be placed in His Holy Word?

"Let them shout for joy, and be glad, that favour my *righteous* cause: yea, let them say continually, Let the Lord be magnified, which hath *pleasure in the prosperity of his servant.*"

> Think about that. Your Heavenly Father is pleased when you prosper, and He's not pleased — He is displeased — when you're not prospering.

If prospering financially in this lifetime were such a shameful and selfish desire, surely God, Himself, would not go to the effort He did to publish the fact that He takes pleasure in prospering His people.

What's more, if God takes such pleasure in prospering His "servants," imagine how much more He would delight in blessing you as His born-again, covenant child.

Think about that. Your Heavenly Father is pleased when you do prosper, and He's not pleased — He is *displeased* — when you're not prospering. Why? Because it gives glory, praise and honor to your Daddy when you're doing well. He's the one that gave it to you, so it's a reflection on Him.

Money in the Right Hands

Once you really start getting all the *truth* about God's attitude and provision for your financial and material well-being deeply imbedded into your spirit, then you will be able to deal with the demonic warfare that has been waged against the Church for centuries.

Satan may be a fool, but he's not stupid. He knew a long time ago the kind of power money would be in the anointed hands of God-fearing believers like you and me. So, he began assaulting the spirituality of money by trying to bring reproach against it in hopes of chasing the Church away from it. And, in part, his scheme worked. Otherwise, you wouldn't have a broke Church running around saying:

> *Satan may be a fool, but he's not stupid. He knew a long time ago the kind of power money would be in the anointed hands of God-fearing believers like you and me.*

"Oh, no, we just couldn't touch any of that unrighteous mammon. That's not our business. That's the world's business. We're too busy being holy."

All the while, however, the Word says that a righteous man is supposed to be wealthy.

It is wrong, even ungodly, to think that a Christian cannot be financially free and financially prosperous. That kind of thinking does not even agree with the Bible.

My friend, you are packing an anointing that can and will blow every curse out of your life, never to be seen again. But you have to give that anointing a chance. More than that, your financial freedom, according to your covenant, will call for out right spiritual warfare. You are going to have to do spiritual warfare to get free, and you are going to have to do spiritual warfare within the Body of Christ.

The Lord is commissioning us, today, as He did the prophet Jeremiah hundreds of years ago:

"Then the Lord put forth his hand, and touched my mouth. And the Lord said unto me, Behold, I have put my words in thy mouth. See, I have this day set thee over the nations and over the kingdoms, to root out, and to pull down, and to destroy, and to throw down, to build, and to plant" (Jeremiah 1:9-10)

Through the Body of Christ, God is in the process of rooting out, pulling down, destroying, throwing down, building and planting. You might call it covenant financial spiritual construction.

Some wrong thinking and some devil-inspired ideas about money have to be rooted out, pulled down, thrown down and destroyed. At the same time, some right thinking and some God-inspired ideas about money, about prosperity, about financial freedom, about how you give and to whom you give need to be planted and built up. . . in your mind and in life.

There's a war out there, my friend. It's a war over your financial freedom. The good news is,

Jesus sanctified you and made you holy—and holy people are supposed to have wealth and riches.

Beware the Con Games

7 chapter

Beware the Con Games

How many times have you given money under pressure?

Perhaps you received a letter from some ministry in the mail, you saw a Christian TV broadcast, you attended a church service or meeting, and you gave because you felt a little pressure in some way to give.

I've been in that sort of situation plenty of times myself and have given thousands of dollars, and I can guarantee you that it wasn't the Holy Spirit nudging me to plant seed into those particular ministers or ministries. It was usually some guilt trip, not God. Consequently, I never saw any harvest on the seed I planted.

Over the years, being in situations like that has become especially challenging because I've been behind the platform before and after services. I've been behind the stage and the curtains where ministers gather. And in many of those places, I've heard a lot of talk about strategies for raising money, strategies that I would call financial rape.

I understand that those words may sound strong, but they are true.

Rape is a violation of another person's private desires. It's forcing or tricking someone into doing something they don't want to do. And the Lord has told me that there is a lot of it going on in the Body of Christ where our money is concerned.

People simply give offerings in response to pressure or manipulation, and then wonder why they're not getting blessed in return. It's because they are not giving under the unction or direction of the Holy Spirit. They're merely playing into the hands of a con game.

That's why in the closing pages of this book, I want to expose some of these different con games, as well as show you ways to avoid them.

Attacking Lack, Attracting Wealth

One morning as I sat on my front porch preparing to read my daily scripture, the Lord brought me to a passage in 1 Kings 13 that would soon serve to protect me, my assignment and the message on financial freedom that I've been sharing with you in these pages.

It would come to guard me against con games.

First Kings 13 opens with a young prophet from Judah going before the altar in Bethel and declaring a word from the Lord:

"O altar, altar, thus saith the Lord; Behold, a child shall be born unto the house of David, Josiah

> *As a prophet of God, I have been crying against the rape being committed by ministers of the gospel against the Body of Christ.*

by name; and upon thee shall he offer the priests of the high places that burn incense upon thee, and men's bones shall be burnt upon thee. And he gave a sign the same day, saying, This is the sign which the Lord hath spoken; Behold, the altar shall be rent, and the ashes that are upon it shall be poured out" (verses 2-3).

As a prophet of God, I have been crying against this rape being committed by ministers of the gospel against the Body of Christ. Because, while we've been so busy worrying about ministers taking our money, one of the major problems I have discovered is ministers not telling people the whole truth.

People have been tithing, giving, believing God, yet they still don't have the financial portfolio they should have. I believe it's because their ministers have been holding back.

While many ministries are in just as bad financial circumstances as the people in their congregations, a lot of the larger ministries are prospering greatly, yet, they never let anyone see it. They teach the principles of financial prosperity, but they are not willing to go public and encourage the Body of Christ that those principles work.

I know those principles work. They work in my life and ministry, so I go around teaching the truth about it all and bragging on God every chance I get — and why not? It's the Lord's doing, not Leroy Thompson's.

You may recall Hosea 4:6, which says, "My people are destroyed for lack of knowledge: because thou hast rejected knowledge, I will also reject thee, that thou shalt be no priest to me: seeing thou hast forgotten the law of thy God, I will also forget thy children."

Those are strong words from the Lord, but consider what's really happening here.

> *In recent years, I have watched as ministers stepped out and started preaching biblical principles of financial prosperity.*

In recent years, I have watched as ministers stepped out and started preaching biblical principles of financial prosperity. Pretty soon those truths started taking hold in the ministers' hearts and minds, and before long the ministers themselves were prospering.

Then, something would happen. Something might be said about them. Suddenly, these ministers would start backing down.

"Oh, well, it was just a move of God through the Church, anyway. It was just a passing wave that won't be around long."

Prosperity, healing, deliverance, speaking in tongues, salvation — those are not passing cycles. They are different aspects of our eternal covenant with God. They're not going anywhere. We just have to press in and stay with it in faith until we get our breakthrough.

Think about it. If there is no hope in the Church for these. . . then there is no hope. . . period.

So, suddenly, you have all these preachers speaking out against this and speaking out against that.

Meanwhile, they're all out of debt and walking in abundance, but their congregations are still left wondering how they are going to make it to the end of the month. That's not right. It's certainly not God. It's a con game.

Remember, what Hosea prophesied?

"Because thou hast rejected knowledge, I will also reject thee, that thou shalt be no priest to me."

The Lord once told me, *He who attacks lack will attract wealth. . . He who attacks wealth will attract lack.*

That's His Word on the matter.

A New Prophet in Town

As we read down into verse 4 of 1 Kings 13, we find that Israel's King Jeroboam happened to be standing by the altar when this young prophet cried out against the altar. When the king heard the word of the Lord, "he put forth his hand from the altar, saying, Lay hold on him. And his hand, which he put forth against [the prophet], dried up, so that he could not pull it in again to him."

In this, the Lord is saying that those who come against this message of prosperity, their finances will be dried up. Their hands will be empty.

The Lord will no longer tolerate His people being held captive financially, not when He already paid the price for them to be free. He will no longer tolerate so called ministers of the gospel coming against His message of prosperity and trying to shut it down.

With that, verses 5-6 tell us:

"The altar also was rent, and the ashes poured out from the altar, according to the sign which the man of God had given by the word of the Lord. And the king answered and said unto the man of God, Intreat now the face of the Lord thy God, and pray for me, that my hand may be restored me again. And the man of God besought the Lord, and the king's hand was restored him again, and became as it was before."

In the same way, many who speak against God prospering His people will be convicted and say, "I've spoken against you. Will you forgive me? I was wrong. Can you help me? I'm broke and my ministry is going under. Will you pray for my restoration?"

Verse 7-10 go on to say:

> **"And the king said unto the man of God, Come home with me, and refresh thyself, and I will give thee a reward. And the man of God said unto the king, If thou wilt give me half thine house, I will not go in with**

thee, neither will I eat bread nor drink water in this place: For so was it charged me by the word of the Lord, saying, Eat no bread, nor drink water, nor turn again by the same way that thou camest. So he went another way, and returned not by the way that he came to Bethel."

The Lord gave this young prophet specific instructions. He charged him not to eat, not to drink, not to go home the same way he had come. These details may seem insignificant to us, but the Word says that our faith should not stand in the wisdom of men, but in the power of God (1 Corinthians 2:5).

This passage, as well as walking in God's system of financial blessing, is all about learning how to discern, how to move in the Spirit. The anointing inside you teaches you all things. It will check you, correct you, direct you, and it will stop you when you need to be stopped. But when you go by emotion, feelings, and the crowd, you are going to move when you should not be moving.

You are not going to get out of debt by running down to every altar to give offerings when the Lord didn't tell you to do it. No, you will end up more in debt.

Keep Your Antenna Up

After all this word from the Lord and supernatural activity had happened with the young prophet from Judah and the King of Israel, an old prophet, who happened to live in Bethel, got wind of it all and jumped on his donkey to pay the new prophet in town a visit.

Verses 14-18:

And went after the man of God, and found him sitting under an oak: and he said unto him, Art thou the man of God that camest from Judah? And he said, I am. Then he said unto him, Come home with me, and

eat bread. And he said, I may not return with thee, nor go in with thee: neither will I eat bread nor drink water with thee in this place: For it was said to me by the word of the Lord, Thou shalt eat no bread nor drink water there, nor turn again to go by the way that thou camest. He said unto him, I am a prophet also as thou art; and an angel spake unto me by the word of the Lord, saying, Bring him back with thee into thine house, that he may eat bread and drink water. But he lied unto him.

Yes, you are to respect your elders. But "old"— even "old prophet"—does not mean right. What's more, you cannot judge by someone's position, title, robes, degrees, etc. There's no revelation from heaven in any of those.

Also, notice that if Satan cannot get you one way, he will try another. . . and another. That's why you cannot let anyone else be in control of you.

The devil will use someone close, someone you respect, and if you are not careful and always on the discerning mode, that someone will be your down fall. And that's what happened here.

Verses 19-24:

> So he went back with him, and did eat bread in his house, and drank water.
>
> And it came to pass, as they sat at the table, that the word of the Lord came unto the prophet that brought him back. And he cried unto the man of God that came from Judah, saying, Thus saith the Lord, Forasmuch as thou hast disobeyed the mouth of the Lord, and hast not kept the commandment which they Lord thy God commanded thee, but camest back, and hast eaten bread and drunk water in the place, of the which the Lord did say to thee, Eat no bread, and drink no water; thy carcase shall not come unto the sepulcher of thy fathers.

And it came to pass, after he had eaten bread, and after he had drunk, that he saddled for him the ass, to wit, for the prophet whom he had brought back. And when he was gone, a lion met him by the way, and slew him: and his carcase was cast in the way, and the ass stood by it, the lion also stood by the carcase.

Undoubtedly, the old prophet somewhere along the way failed to hear and obey God himself. He chose to go along with what King Jeroboam was doing, which was sure not to be of God. God probably had tried to get the old prophet to go to the king and stop all this mess. But, instead, he went along with the status quo. So, God had to call a prophet from the outside to do his job.

In the end, the old prophet recognized and honored the young prophet as a man of God.

Practicing Dollars and Sense

Financial freedom requires each of us as believers to discern what is, and is not, from God. If we were to always give when someone asked for something, or told us to give, we all would be out of money.

"Well, praise God, I gave my last hundred dollars."

Don't give your hundred dollars if the Lord didn't tell you to give it. Check it out with Him, first. You may need to use that money to pay your electricity bill.

That's like the man who gave his car away because he saw someone else do it. He's not going to be driving a new car to work next week. He's going to be walking, or catching a ride with someone else because he didn't hear from God.

In light of that, there are three guidelines the Spirit of God gave me to warn the Body of Christ about when it comes to our sowing financial seed:

First, don't sow your seed in the wrong place. Too many Christians are giving their money away, putting it in the wrong place at the wrong time and they are not going to receive a harvest from it.

Instead, pray and ask the Spirit what you should do. Then detect, or discern, by the Spirit where you are to sow the seed you do have. It's more important to know what to do with a seed, than to know how much seed you have.

Second, don't sow your seed in the wrong person or ministry.

There are actually ministers and ministries that are not whole-heartedly pursuing your best interest, namely your prosperity. They're mostly concerned about their own prosperity. They want you to do all the sowing. Meanwhile, they don't teach you about sowing and reaping. They just come up with a couple scriptures to try and manipulate you into giving.

Matthew 4:20 reminds us that our seed must be sown on good ground in order to produce "some thirty fold, some sixty, and some an hundred."

So don't just drop your money in an offering plate, or whatever, as though you were plunking it in a slot machine.

So don't just drop your money in an offering plate, or whatever, as though you were plunking it in a slot machine. . . just taking a chance. Hear from God, first. Then sow purposefully into good soil, realizing that good soil is soil that produces. And if a particular minister or ministry has not touched your life in some noticeable way, then there probably is no anointing on their ministry for your life. So, move on.

The third guideline to watch for is sowing for the wrong purposes.

Don't give out of excitement, or out of emotions. Purpose to hear from God, and then do what He tells you to do.

A minister called me one time asking for a certain amount of money he needed to keep a ministry project from going down the tubes. I listened to his request, then told him I would pray about it. I had the money to give the man, and I really would like to have given it to him. But here's what the Lord told me:

Don't you try to take my place. A lot of times I am teaching a person a lesson and here you come because I have blessed you and you can do it and you come and give it to them and now the whole lesson is gone and you have become their source.

It all comes down to knowing when to sow and when not to sow. God can trust you with money once you've learned when and where to sow.

Your Are Here!

The first law in reading a map is that you have to find out where you are before you can figure out where you're going. And that's exactly what I have purposed to do in this book.

I want to help you locate yourself. I want to help set your sites on your covenant with God. . . so you can get to that higher place He has for all of us financially. As I've said before my intent and my ministry is not about getting money *from* you. It's about getting money *to* you (Philippians 4:14-18).

Maybe you've already discovered in reading this book that you have become too accustomed to financial pressures — juggling a mortgage, car payments and credit cards, in an economy threatened by recession. Well, you're not alone.

I'm reminded of the pressures King David faced long before he was ever crowned king.

First Samuel 22:1-2 tells us that after David fled the threat of King Saul and escaped to a cave, he was joined by a band of followers described as "every one that was *in distress,* and every one that was *in debt,* and every one that was *discontented.*"

Then it says that they all "gathered themselves unto him; and he became a captain over them: and there were with him about four hundred men."

I don't know about you, but I'm prone to think these guys were under some financial pressures. Yet, they had the courage to come together and start somewhere.

As I've said before, it's important to get honest with yourself, and get honest with God. Just start right where you are and open your heart to God. He will do the rest.

One of the instructors from our School of Ministry once gave me a statement that put into words what I was seeing God do in the Body of Christ to help us develop in our financial steward-ship in these last days. This is what it said:

God first works in the life of another and works thoroughly so he may give that person, to you as an authority above you for you to learn obedience and to possess what you have never possessed before. This man's wealth becomes your wealth. Should you overlook this divine procedure, though

you may live for 50 years, you may lag far behind the attainment of that person.

The way God grants his grace, to us is two-fold, sometimes — though rarely — He grants grace to us directly. Mostly, He gives His riches to us indirectly. That is, God puts above you those who are more advance spiritually so you may accept their judgment as your judgment. This will then enable you to possess the wealth without you, yourself, having to go through their painful experience.

To rebel is to choose the way of poverty.

The point of this statement is that God is sending leaders and pioneers before you—no differently than he did in King David's day.

But if you are going to receive the full benefit of the principles and trails those pioneers are blazing for you, then you must not rebel against the revelation that is divinely connected or associated with those benefits.

Instead, receive those revelations from heaven. Receive *"I'll never be broke another day in my life!"* as your Word from God. As you do, God will see to it that those revelations manifest in a physical sense, not just the spiritual.

Other Books by Dr. Leroy Thompson, Sr.

Money Thou Art Loosed!

How To Find Your Wealthy Place

Money Cometh to the Body of Christ!

Framing Your World with the Word of God

The Voice of Jesus:
Speaking God's Word with Authority

Money with A Mission

What To Do When Your Faith is Challenged

To Order,
Write or Call:

Ever Increasing Word Ministries
P.O. Box 7
Darrow, LA 70725

1-888-238-WORD
(9673)

Order Online at:

WWW.EIWM.ORG

To contact Dr. Leroy Thompson Sr.,
write:

Dr. Leroy Thompson Sr.
Ever Increasing Word Ministries
P.O. Box 7
Darrow, LA 70725

Please include your prayer requests
and comments when you write.

To obtain a free catalog of Dr. Thompson's teaching materials
or to receive a free quarterly newsletter, write to the address above.